ALICE'S ADVENTURES IN OXFORD

Mavis Batey tells the story of Alice Liddell, the daughter of the Dean of Christ Church, and the immortal friendship with 'Lewis Carroll', the mathematics don, which inspired the Alice books.

Mrs Batey, who is married to the Treasurer of Christ Church, has made a special study of the Oxford background to the famous Alice stories, which throws a new and refreshing light on Lewis Carroll as child-lover and gifted story-teller.

*   *   *

'She saw an ancient city, and a quiet river winding near it along the plain, and up the stream went slowly gliding a boat with a merry party of children on board – she could hear their voices and laughter like music over the water'. From Alice's Adventures Under Ground. The water-colour is by J. M. W. Turner, as is that on page 3; the photograph of Alice is by Charles Dodgson.

ALICE'S ADVENTURES IN OXFORD

Mavis Batey

Alice in Wonderland and Lewis Carroll belong to Oxford. She was the daughter of the Dean of Christ Church and he was one of the college tutors. Alice was born in 1852 at Westminster School, where her father, the Revd Henry George Liddell, was head master. She was four years old when the family moved to the Deanery at Christ Church. The rest of the family then consisted of her brother Harry, aged nine, and two sisters, Lorina, who was six, and Edith two years old. The first record of her meeting Lewis Carroll is an entry in his diary in 1856: 'April 25. (F). Went over with Southey in the afternoon to the Deanery, to try and take a photograph of the Cathedral: both attempts proved failures. The three little girls were in the garden most of the time, and we became excellent friends: we tried to group them in the foreground of the picture, but they were not patient sitters. I mark this day with a white stone'. The 'white stone' in his diary was reserved for days which Lewis Carroll felt would have particular significance in his life. He did not guess that this day marked the beginning of a child friendship which was to inspire one of the most famous books in the world. The shared experiences of Lewis Carroll and Alice in Oxford would be relived in a Wonderland and Looking Glass world to the delight of generations of young and old alike.

Charles Dodgson, as Lewis Carroll was in real life, arrived at Christ Church as an undergraduate on 24 January 1851 at the age of 19 and, except for vacations, remained there for the rest of his life. He took a first class degree in mathematics, was elected to a Studentship (the equivalent of a fellowship in other colleges), was ordained deacon, became a member of the Governing Body and for nine years was Curator of the Common Room. The House, as the cathedral college, or *Aedes Christi*, is known in Oxford, was both home and a way of life for Charles Dodgson for 47 years. 'However it may be for others', he protested, when the House of Commons was referred to as The House in his hearing, 'for us there can only be one house – the House for us is Christ Church'.

*   *   *

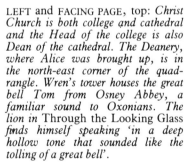

LEFT and FACING PAGE, top: *Christ Church is both college and cathedral and the Head of the college is also Dean of the cathedral. The Deanery, where Alice was brought up, is in the north-east corner of the quadrangle. Wren's tower houses the great bell Tom from Osney Abbey, a familiar sound to Oxonians. The lion in* Through the Looking Glass *finds himself speaking 'in a deep hollow tone that sounded like the tolling of a great bell'.*

FACING PAGE, bottom left: *Charles Lutwidge Dodgson (1832–98). This portrait in the Great Hall of Christ Church was painted posthumously by Herkomer from a photograph. The pseudonym 'Lewis Carroll', first used for the poem* Solitude, *was derived from his mother's maiden name Lutwidge, the German for Lewis, and the Latin for Charles – Carolus.*

FACING PAGE, bottom right: *Dean Liddell (1811–98). A 'nobly presenced Dean . . . young ladies delightful; prelate prelatic' wrote Ruskin. While admiring his rare qualities, Dodgson did not always feel at ease with Alice's father.*

3

Alice, as the daughter of the Head of the House, naturally grew up with similar loyalties. 'We must burn the house down', said the Rabbit's voice, and Alice called out as loud as she could, 'If you do, I'll set Dinah at you.'

To the casual observer Charles Dodgson was a typical, rather reserved Oxford don, who gave lectures in mathematics, attended meetings and occasionally published university pamphlets. When the fairy tales he wrote for Alice

Liddell became famous he shrank from the publicity that the acknowledged authorship would have brought him. In later years letters addressed to Lewis Carroll, Christ Church, Oxford were returned to the Post Office 'not known', and the Bodleian Library received a sharp rebuke for a catalogue entry linking Charles Dodgson the author of *An Elementary Treatise on Determinants* with Lewis Carroll the author of *Alice's Adventures in Wonderland.* Many people in Oxford did know his secret, of course, and eagerly awaited fresh masterpieces of nonsense from Christ Church. 'No it is not funny – it's about Euclid', was the firm reply to the hopeful enquiry of a lady who called on him one afternoon when he was engrossed in writing a new book.

Charles Dodgson was happiest and most relaxed in the company of children. Colleagues got used to the procession of children up to his rooms, first in one of the cloister staircases and then in Tom Quad. His inventiveness began in his own rectory childhood in the north of England, when he provided entertainment for his seven sisters: a marionette theatre, a family maga-

*   *   *

LEFT: *The Chestnut Tree in the Deanery garden. The Cheshire cat sat on a similar horizontal bough (see front cover). Alice's real tabby cat who sat upon the Deanery tree was called Dinah; it had been given to Lorina but became Alice's special cat to which she was devoted.*

FACING PAGE: *The Library. Charles Dodgson was sub-librarian from 1855–57 and worked in a room overlooking the Deanery garden, where the Liddell children were at play. Dinah often had to be retrieved from the library. Dodgson first made friends with Alice and her sisters when he was photographing the cathedral from the Deanery garden. He later took many photographs of Lorina, Alice and Edith in the garden, told them stories and invented a game called Croquet Castles for them, which was published in 1863.*

zine, conjuring tricks and all manner of games, puzzles and gadgets. His rooms in Christ Church were said to resemble a toy-shop, but slide rules and musical boxes never got muddled up. He was extremely tidy and methodical and there was a place for everything. Bob the Bat always lived in the top left drawer of the writing desk, and he and the mechanical bear with glaring eyes were great favourites with child visitors. One day Bob, who was an ingenious creation of gauze, wire and elastic, flew right out of the window and landed on a tray a scout (college servant) was taking up to a neighbour's rooms, giving the poor man such a fright that he dropped it and broke a salad bowl into pieces.

A treasured ornament in Charles Dodgson's rooms was a tiny monocular into which a photograph of the young Alice Liddell and her sisters Lorina and Edith was permanently set.

Charles Dodgson was an accomplished photographer, and he kept a dressing-room with a cupboard full of fancy costumes for his child friends. Alice recalled that it was more fun to watch him develop the large glass plates than actually to be photographed, which was rather a lengthy process. When he had rooms in Tom Quad overlooking St Aldate's, he obtained permission to build a studio on the roof. The roof itself was a great attraction, and children were invited up to watch

civic processions to the Town Hall and were allowed to play hide-and-seek amongst the chimney pots. One little girl was even given a hammer to strike Great Tom, which must have confused the time-conscious Oxonians. 'Don't children ever bore you?' asked an incredulous undergraduate. 'Little children are three-fourths of my life, I don't see how they could bore anyone,' was the bachelor don's sincere reply.

Although make-believe and mathematics had to be kept apart, there was no personality split between Dodgson the don and clergyman and Carroll the inventor of fairy tales; his imaginative writing, logical mind, religious faith

Continued on page 8

FACING PAGE, top left: *Dodgson's photographic equipment in the Museum of the History of Science in Oxford.*

FACING PAGE, bottom left: *Dodgson's diary for 28 March 1863 reads: 'Went to Rejlander's (the photographer) and got my picture taken, large and small and half length. I also 'looked over a large number of prints and negatives, some of which were very beautiful'. The other photographs on the facing page are by Dodgson: Prince Leopold, the youngest son of Queen Victoria, who was a student at Christ Church; and a charming study made in 1857 of the daughter of an employee at Croft Rectory. Dodgson delighted to photograph little girls, a subject at which he excelled.*

ABOVE: *A family group taken by Dodgson at Croft Rectory in 1857 – six of his sisters and his youngest brother Edwin.*

RIGHT: *The Misses Lutwidge, two of Dodgson's maiden aunts, photographed by their nephew c.1860.*

and love of children were all of a piece. A delight in make-believe may seem inconsistent with a logical mind, but his imaginative genius was a unique brand of fun-loving nonsense based on logic which appealed instantly to children, especially to an observant, enquiring child like Alice. Many of the naïve remarks in his stories were Alice's own, or treasured memories of what he had heard other children say in trains, public parks and at the seaside. For example, the Professor's remark in *Sylvie and Bruno Concluded* that 'it doesn't bite at that end' he had actually heard a child say when warned of the danger he was incurring by pulling a dog's tail.

One child friend recalled how 'Mr Dodgson' took delight in the absurdity of the common misuse of words, and loved to lead children through the most complicated mazes of reasoning to the conclusion that they had meant exactly the opposite of what they had said. Alice, who was an adept at asking challenging and disconcerting questions, enjoyed such teasing and the kind of logical argument in *Through the Looking Glass* when the Messenger says in a sullen tone: 'I'm sure nobody walks much faster than I do', and the King replies: 'He can't do that or else he'd have been here first.'

The meanings of words fascinated Charles Dodgson as they did many of the argumentative, donnish creatures in the Alice books. The exchange between Alice and the Frog is an example of the nonsense based on word-play which delighted both the child and the logician. 'Where's the servant whose business it is to answer the door?', she began . . . 'To answer the door?' he said. 'What's it been asking of?' Charles Dodgson could not resist making capital out of word-ambiguity even on solemn occasions, and once when the opportunity presented itself on the occasion of the appointment of a Professor of Philology he was unable to contain himself. After he had listened for some time to a member of Convocation declaring with much eloquence that the chief duty of so great a university was to turn out as many good professors as possible, the creator of Humpty Dumpty sprang to his feet and called out: 'Quite right! Quite right! Turn them out!'

Alice Liddell, as a lexicographer's daughter, had the same respect for words and approved the sentiment that 'Language is worth a thousand pounds a word'. Her father's famous Greek Lexicon, Liddell and Scott, had paid for the beautiful new Gothic stairs at the Deanery, which she and her sisters had christened the 'Lexicon Stairs'. The dictionary continued to be a best seller and when Charles Dodgson took Alice round the University Press during one of their walks in 1863 it was being set up for its sixth edition.

These walks round Oxford were full of interest and excitement, especially as the Liddell children were honoured guests at any university institution. Not only was their father a Delegate of the Press, but he was also a Curator of the Bodleian Library, a Delegate of the University Museum and Art Galleries and a Curator of the Chest. Dean Liddell was involved in all the reforms and enterprises which made the Oxford of the 1860s such a lively intellectual centre, and Mrs Liddell was renowned for her evening parties for distinguished guests. The Deanery was not the kind of Victorian household where children were banished to the nursery; Alice and her sisters often stayed up for the parties, listened to the singing or played parlour games with bishops and professors in the long gallery. Alice knew most of the Oxford professors, since they were the only resident members of the University, other than the Heads of Houses and the canons of Christ Church, who were allowed to marry, and most of her friends were professors' children.

Alice was very familiar with Oxford academics who talked like the egg-headed Professor Humpty

* * *

Dumpty or were ready to give philosophical advice like the hookah-smoking caterpillar. Professor Bartholomew Price, who was a great friend and former tutor of Charles Dodgson, was well known at the Deanery. He was always known as 'Bat' in Oxford, which Dodgson conveniently linked with his interest in astronomy for Alice's Wonderland:

'Twinkle, twinkle, little bat!
How I wonder what you're at!
Up above the world you fly,
Like a tea-tray in the sky!'

Like Mr Dodgson's mechanical bat, he had a habit of flying above everybody's heads.

The Liddell children took a lively interest in all that went on in Oxford. The building of the new University Museum and the transfer to it of the material from the Christ Church Museum were discussed as important matters at the Deanery. The museum was finished in time for the famous British Association meeting in Oxford in 1860, when the debate between the Darwinite Huxley and the creationist Wilberforce took place, an event commemorated by a plaque in the Upper West Gallery. Charles Dodgson was on the reception committee for the 'men of science from foreign countries and distant parts of the UK,' and arranged to take a photograph of Huxley while he was in Oxford. His own contribution to the burning question of Natural Selection was the invention of a game of that name in which the winner demonstrated the theory of 'the survival of the fittest'.

FACING PAGE: *Alice and her sister Lorina in Chinese costume, photographed by Dodgson.*

RIGHT: *Alice as a beggar child, a study by Dodgson made in 1858. She was then six and Tennyson said it was the most beautiful photograph of a child he had ever seen.*

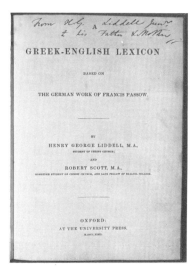

crustaceans, reptiles and insects. A visit to the Insect Gallery is recalled in a *Looking Glass* chapter:

'What sort of insects do you rejoice in, where *you* come from?' the gnat inquired.

'I don't *rejoice* in insects at all' Alice explained . . . 'But I can tell you the names of some of them'.

'What's the use of their having names', the Gnat said, 'if they won't answer to them?'

'No use to *them*' said Alice, 'but it's useful to the people that name them, I suppose'.

Alice thought that it would be better if their stinging habits, rather than their classifications, should be recorded. 'What she really wanted to know was, whether it could sting or not, but she thought this would not be a civil question to ask'.

The ornamentation of the Museum reflected its scientific content. 'Such capitals as we will have!' wrote Ruskin to Acland. 'I hope to get Millais and Rossetti to design flower and beast borders – crocodiles and various vermin – such as you are particularly fond of.' Dodgson's diary records talks with friends on 'Art and Ruskin' and his philosophy of the relationship of art, work and living things. It was indeed an exciting time in Oxford in 1860. The spirit of the Middle Ages was being revived. The Pre-Raphaelites, many of whom Dodgson knew personally, were finishing the paintings and carvings depicting the Arthurian

The University Museum was Oxford's Crystal Palace, a splendid Spirit of the Age building, the brainchild of John Ruskin and Sir Henry Acland, both former pupils of Dean Liddell, who gave their project his whole-hearted support. Acland was the Liddell family doctor, and a lifelong friend of the Dean's. Ruskin was Alice's drawing master. In her Wonderland he appears as 'an old conger eel, that used to come once a week' to teach 'drawling, stretching and fainting in coils'. Alice and her sisters liked to visit the museum with all its stuffed animals and birds, especially if Mr Dodgson was there to make up

stories about the animals. A favourite exhibit in the main hall was the remains of the strange dodo which had first been brought to Oxford in 1683 with the rest of the Tradescant Collection of Rarities. Beside it was the painting by John Savery of 1651, showing a huge dodo which had also been transferred to the new museum from the old Ashmolean Museum in Broad Street. Oxford claimed to have the last remains of a dodo, and it was with this creature that Charles Dodgson chose to identify himself in Alice's Wonderland adventures.

The upstairs galleries housed the Hope collection of tortoises, legends at the Oxford Union. Dodgson's own visual imagination was channelled into his photography, which was a form of artistic expression for him, and his photographs show a Pre-Raphaelite influence.

The installation of the St Frideswide window in the Latin chapel of the cathedral, one of Burne-Jones's first essays in glass painting, was a great event in the world of Pre-Raphaelite art. It was much admired by Dean Liddell, and all Christ Church watched the assembling of the stained glass on the grass behind the cathedral. Alice had been brought up on the story of Oxford's patron saint, and took a special interest in the scenes in the life of the Saxon princess depicted in the window. She had learned her 'drawling and stretching' well from the old conger eel, and in later years Ruskin's young pupil herself became a competent artist and an accomplished woodcarver. She carved a door for a new church dedicated to St

* * *

11

fontes aquarum et absterget deus

Frideswide of Oxford, built in Poplar in 1888 for the Christ Church mission, of which her father was chairman. The top panel of the door shows the saint arriving by boat down the Thames to found a monastery on the site of which Christ Church now stands.

St Frideswide's shrine is in the cathedral but legend also associates her with the holy well at Binsey and both places were visited by pilgrims in the Middle Ages. It is said that St Frideswide was pursued to Binsey by King Algar, who wanted to marry her but was struck blind for his boldness. Her prayers to St Margaret called forth a miraculous well whose waters cured her suitor's blindness, and he departed leaving the saint to return to Oxford to found her monastery in peace. The holy well was known as the Treacle Well in Binsey, in its medieval sense of a healing fluid as used in the Treacle Bible. The well became overgrown, and Charles Dodgson's friend, the Revd Thomas Prout, decided to clear it when, in 1857, he became incum-bent of the church there. The story of the Treacle Well was very familiar to Charles Dodgson and duly found its way into Wonder-land.

'Once upon a time there were three little sisters . . . and their names were Elsie, Lacie and Til-lie and they lived at the bottom of a well'.

"Why did they live at the bot-tom of a well?"

'The Dormouse again took a minute or two to think about it and said: "It was a treacle well".

"There's no such thing!" Alice

was beginning very angrily . . .'

Alice had no excuse for doubting the treacle well because she had often seen it on walks to Binsey with her governess, Miss Prickett, whose family lived there. The walks were a necessary part of the children's afternoon routine, since it was a strict rule that they should not run about in the quad and disturb people who were working. They had to let off steam in Christ Church Meadows where they were taken by Miss Prickett. They were delighted when Mr Dodgson was free from his mathematics and could accompany them to Dean's Ham by the river, along the Broad Walk to the Botanic garden and the Cherwell walks, or to see the deer at Magdalen or feed the ducks on the Worcester lake. His rooms in the Cloister Building were near Broad Walk (Meadow Buildings had not yet been built) and he could see them setting off each afternoon.

Charles Dodgson delighted in taking children round Oxford and made up stories about the exciting things they saw. Alice knew all there was to see in Christ Church, but other children began their outings with the medieval hall and kitchen there. The gargoyles were great fun and he always pointed out one particular favourite, a large jolly face at the top of a wall at Magdalen which is being helped to laugh by a little man pulling up the corner of his mouth for him. Dodgson had been fascinated by carvings in his father's

*   *   *

FACING PAGE: *The University Museum – Oxford's Gothic temple of natural science. The stone columns supporting the arcade are geological exhibits, the carved capitals represent a series of plants with birds and rare animals.*

RIGHT: *Alice, aged 21, by Julia Margaret Cameron, a famous Victorian photographer. Dodgson's diary for 24 April 1873 reads: 'Called on the Dean on business, met Mrs Liddell who took me into the drawing room to see photos, where Alice showed me the large ones Mrs Cameron had done of them'.*

churches at Daresbury and Croft, and later, when his father became Archdeacon, with the work of the famous carvers of Ripon, depicting fighting knights, pigs playing bagpipes and lions fighting dragons. Alice pretended that carved lions at the Deanery came alive and chased her. 'Let's pretend' was Alice's favourite phrase, and she was the ideal child friend to stimulate Mr Dodgson's genius for make-believe. He had a lively sense of the dramatic and was a great lover of the theatre and pantomime and an adept at toy theatres. He liked to experiment with dissolving views in magic lantern slides, and when he came to write *Through the Looking Glass* there were episodes in it, such as the Sheep's knitting needles turning into Alice's oars or the egg in the shop enlarging into Humpty Dum-

pty, where he seems to be using the dissolving technique in his writing.

Alice and her sisters often went to college theatricals or extravaganzas in undergraduate rooms, and sometimes saw Mr Dodgson there. Oxford also attracted a number of outside entertainers in term-time and, judging by the advertisements in local papers, the citizens and undergraduates had the benefit of all the best London shows as performed before the crowned heads of Europe. Alice and her sisters sometimes went to circuses and other entertainments with their don friend, or, more often, would go with their governess and tell him all about it at their next meeting. In the two years preceding the writing down of her Adventures, Alice could have seen the Ohio

centre of the story. As Alice herself said, 'the stories grew into new tales owing to the frequent interruptions which opened up fresh and undreamed-of possibilities'. The stories lived and died like summer midges, in Charles Dodgson's words, and the little drawings he made to illustrate a particular character or situation were tossed in the waste-paper basket. 'If you don't know what a gryphon is, look at the picture', the child reader is told in *Alice's Adventures in Wonderland*.

Special treats for Edith, Lorina and Alice, marked with a 'white stone' in Dodgson's diary, were their boating trips on the Thames, or the Isis as it is also called at Oxford. Dodgson would ask one of his friends to accompany him, usually the Revd Robinson Duckworth of Trinity who was famous for his renderings of popular songs; and, because there was no governess to supervise the children, the party was gay and relaxed. They trailed their hands in the water or picked forget-me-nots or Alice's favourite scented rushes from the bank. Sculls were kept in the boat and the children took turns at rowing. It was a proud day when they could 'feather their oars' properly. Sometimes they would head up the river, passing by Binsey and Port Meadow to Godstow, where they would land and boil a kettle of water for tea under a haycock. Sometimes they would go down the river to Iffley and Sandford, or if it was a whole-day excursion, row on to Nuneham Park as a special treat. Their friends the Harcourts provided huts for picnickers in the woods and after the children had chosen the rendezvous for the day, they went off to the cottages in the dingle to borrow plates, glasses, and knives and forks for their cold chicken and salad provided by Charles Dodgson's scout. 'The hut might have been a Fairy King's palace and the picnic a banquet in our honour. Sometimes we were told stories after luncheon that transported us into Fairyland', Alice remembered as an old lady.

On 4 July 1862 a memorable excursion took place, this time up

Continued on page 18

Minstrels singing 'O Beautiful Star', a programme of 'physical and natural magic' called *Two Hours in Wonder World, a Grand Eastern Moving Diorama*, a ventriloquist who performed 'How doth the little busy bee' to perfection, a mesmerist who made people behave like babies or sneeze violently, a conjuror who produced 'Live Flowers in an Enchanted Garden', an electro-biologist who could change the taste of water to vinegar or make people lose their memories, and a sensational Talking Fish. It was

an interesting background for the storybook Alice who lost her memory, changed her size, talked to Live Flowers and heard Humpty Dumpty send messages to the fish.

'Tell us a story!' was the constant cry of the Dean's daughters whenever they met Mr Dodgson. His great gift as a story-teller was that he wove the story round the child's experiences, making of them a fantastic Wonderland, but taking care to follow where their imaginations suggested, so that the child always remained at the

ABOVE: *Dodgson's sitting room. He moved into the elegant suite of rooms overlooking St Aldates in 1868. Instructions for lighting the elaborate gaselier were pasted on the door. An entry in his diary for 4 March 1887 refers to the tiles surrounding the fireplace: 'Called on Mr William de Morgan and chose a set of red tiles for the large fireplace'. Mr Dodgson interpreted the tiles for his child visitors as the Lory, the Dodo, the Fawn, the Eaglet and the Gryphon from Alice in Wonderland. After his death they were removed from the fireplace and made into the fire screen seen on the facing page.*

*

RIGHT: *Dodgson's advertisement for his brother's marmalade when he was curator of the Common Room. It was offered at 9d or 10d a pot. Alice we are told 'always took a great interest in questions of eating and drinking' and was particularly fond of orange marmalade. Oxford, of course, is noted for a famous brand of orange marmalade.*

15

82

Christ Church, Oxford.

To all Lovers of Orange Marmalade.

The Curator's brother, (who has a large family and several pupils) makes it on a large scale, and could supply some for the use of Members of C.R., if any let the Curator know that they desire it. He finds it very good, and it can also be guaranteed as absolutely

FACING PAGE: *The Binsey Treacle Well, a place for pilgrimages in the Middle Ages, a scene from the St Frideswide window in the Latin Chapel in Christ Church Cathedral. It is by Burne-Jones and was executed in 1859. His signpost is misleading – Oxford and Binsey are in the same direction from the holy well.*

ABOVE: *The Dodo, the extinct bird which inspired the famous character. In Alice's Adventures in Wonderland Dodgson was the Dodo. This painting by John Savery is in the University Museum. Oxford has the last remains of the dodo which came from the Tradescant Collection of Rarities in Lambeth, London.*

RIGHT: *Charles Dodgson, aged 23, by an unknown photographer.*

the river to Godstow. The excited Liddell children hurried round the quad from the Deanery, to Mr Dodgson's new rooms in the north-west corner (now completely changed into the Junior Common Room). He had changed his gown for white flannels and a straw hat and he and Duckworth carried the picnic basket and kettle down the path by the Trill Mill stream to Salter's boat yard with Edith, Lorina and Alice skipping along beside them. As they rowed away with Duckworth as stroke, Alice as cox and Mr Dodgson as bow, and Tom Tower and the cathedral spire faded from sight, he picked up the threads of the interminable story of Alice's Adventures in which Alice was the heroine, her sisters Lorina and Edith the Lory and the Eaglet, Duckworth the Duck and Dodgson himself the Dodo. The story had ended in a soaking when they had been to Nuneham a few weeks before, and had been caught in a downpour. Mr Dodgson had taken them ashore, 'a curious-looking party that assembled on the bank', to dry off in a friend's lodgings at Sandford and to get a gig to take them back to Oxford. 'If the Dodo hadn't known the way to that nice little cottage, I don't know when we should have got dry again', said Alice. The story on 4 July began with Alice going down a rabbit hole. The children lay back on the comfy cushions and listened, but suddenly to tease

*   *   *

ABOVE LEFT: *The top panel carved by Alice of a door made for the Poplar Mission Church, illustrating an episode in the life of St Frideswide, patron saint of Oxford. The Mission church was destroyed by bombing during the war, but the door was saved and is now at St Frideswide's, Osney.*

LEFT: *Alice and the story-book deer. The Liddell children delighted in walking with Dodgson in Magdalen Deer Park.*

FACING PAGE: *It was probably at Godstow that Alice saw the wicker eel traps featured in Tenniel's Father William illustration. They were a common sight on Thames weirs in those days. The contemporary sketch is from a book of scenes of the Thames.*

18

ABOVE: *Wolsey's great kitchen at Christ Church, drawn by Augustus Pugin for Ackerman's* History of Oxford, *1814. 'The door led to a large kitchen, which was full of smoke from one end to the other'. From the Pig and Pepper episode,* Alice's Adventures in Wonderland.

LEFT: *Alice in the Sheep Shop where she bought her favourite barley sugar. The window and the door are reversed in position by Tenniel as though seen Through the Looking Glass.*

FACING PAGE: *The Sheep Shop in St Aldates today. It is now known as 'The Alice in Wonderland Shop'.*

FACING PAGE, inset: *The Magdalen Gargoyle. 'At the top of the wall in one corner they saw a very large jolly face carved in stone, with a broad grin, and a little man at the side helping him to laugh by pulling up the corners of his mouth for him. 'Isa thought that the next time she wants to laugh, she will get Nellie and Maggie to help her'. From* Isa's Visit to Oxford.

20

them or perhaps because he too was getting drowsy in the heat of the afternoon – Charles Dodgson said 'And that's all till next time'. 'Ah, but it is next time,' they cried and with some persuasion Alice's Adventures Underground started up again.

The day was to have an important ending for these stories were not to die like summer midges. When Alice bade her friends goodnight on the Deanery doorstep she said, 'Oh, Mr Dodgson, I wish you would write out Alice's adventures for me'. According to Duckworth, Dodgson sat up nearly the whole night writing down what he could remember to please Alice. The next day he had planned a trip to the International Exhibition at Kensington, and on the 9.02 train to London he jotted down the chapter headings for Alice's book. Her ambition that 'there ought to be a book written about me that there ought' was not achieved until the end of 1864, when she received the finished version of *Alice's Adventures Under Ground* as a 'Christmas present to a Dear Child in memory of a Summer's day' in her don-friend's neat handwriting with his own illustrations.

Friends in Oxford who saw the manuscript urged him to publish it, but he was unwilling to believe that the stories about Alice and her sisters, interspersed with the songs, games and jokes they had shared, would be of general interest. The book was sent to his friend, George Macdonald, a writer of children's stories, with the request that he would try out his own children's reaction to Alice's Adventures. Young Greville was so enthusiastic in his praises, saying he wished there were

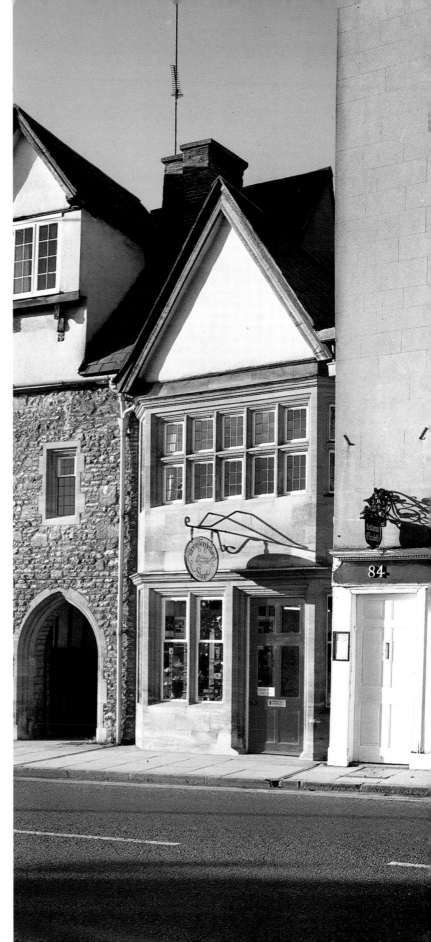

60,000 volumes of it, that Charles Dodgson was persuaded to publish a revised edition of the book with professional illustrations. He had hoped that with tuition his own illustrating would improve, but when Ruskin advised him that his talent was not sufficient to merit devoting much time to it, he approached the Punch artist John Tenniel, whose drawings of animals for Aesop's Fables had appealed to him. There could have been no better choice than John Tenniel; indeed it is difficult to think of Alice without Tenniel's line drawings, so perfectly do they match the Carroll imagination. Tenniel was brought down to Oxford to see the background and was given minute instructions as to what was required and the publishers, Macmillans, were told exactly how to set his drawings in the text. It was agreed that the heroine's face should not be a likeness of the real Alice, but details of her dress were carefully supervised. 'Don't give Alice so much crinoline', was one of the numerous messages Tenniel received as work progressed.

The first copy of *Alice's Adventures in Wonderland*, the new title suggested by Dean Liddell, was sent to Alice on 4 July, 1865, three years to the day after the river trip which had inspired the book. Many other stories told to Alice and her sisters over the years which could not be included in *Alice's Adventures in Wonderland* were held in reserve. *Through the Looking Glass* was, therefore, written with publication in mind, unlike the first volume of Alice, and has a much more sophisticated plot within the framework of a game of chess. It is also more nostalgic than *Wonderland* because by the time Lewis Carroll came to write down his 'floating idea' for *Through the Looking Glass and What Alice Found There*, Alice had long ceased to visit her don friend and to beg for stories. She was 19 years old, with her hair up, when she received the first copy of the book, bound in morocco, on 18 December 1871.

Through the Looking Glass has a very special setting. The year was 1863, the year of the wedding of the Prince of Wales (later Edward VII) to Princess Alexandra of Denmark, and the book begins

*　　*　　*

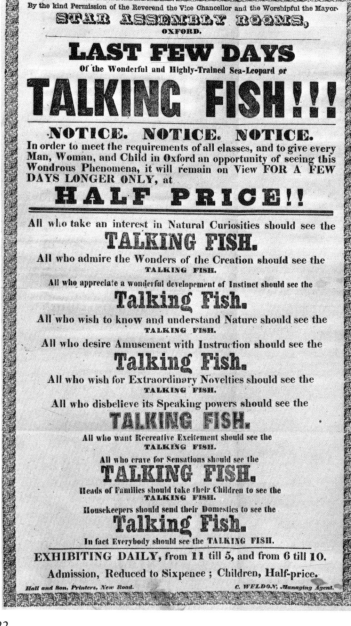

LEFT: *The playbill announcing the visit of the Talking Fish to Oxford, April 1863. All would-be entertainers had to obtain permission both from the Mayor and the Vice-Chancellor and many of their bills are preserved in the University archives.*

FACING PAGE, above: *Nuneham Park showing the Carfax Conduit, owned by an uncle of Dodgson's Christ Church friend, Augustus Vernon-Harcourt, the scene of many a happy picnic for the Liddell children.*

FACING PAGE, below: *'For the Duchess. An invitation from The Queen to play croquet'. Alice was invited to play croquet with the Royals when they stayed at the Deanery. Shortly before a splendid Talking Fish had visited Oxford (see playbill).*

with Alice playing 'Let's pretend we're kings and queens' with her sister. The Illuminations in Oxford to celebrate the wedding day on 10 March and the visit of the royal newly-weds to the Deanery in Commemoration Week play a part comparable to the Godstow picnic in *Alice's Adventures in Wonderland*; both were highlights in Alice's life. Alice had been determined to do the full tour of the Oxford Illuminations, bonfires and fireworks and took the matter in hand herself. She sent a note round to Mr Dodgson's room asking him to escort her round the town. His brother was staying with him at the time, but he was only too pleased to comply with Alice's request. It was a memorable evening. Dodgson recorded in his diary that it was 'delightful to see the thorough abandonment with which Alice enjoyed the whole thing'. The Wedding Day of the Prince of Wales was, of course, marked with a 'white stone'. Alice, for her part, was to remember all her life, the fun of that evening, when she had clung to Dodgson's hand and they had made up stories about those Illuminations which had specially taken their fancy. Much of the

Continued on page 26

23

for I never was as small as this be[fore,]
never! And I declare it's too bad, it [is!]

At this mome[nt]
her foot slipp[ed,]
and splash! [she]
was up to her [chin]
in salt water. [Her]
first idea w[as]
that she ha[d]
fallen into [the]
sea: then s[he]
remembered t[hat]
she was und[er]
ground, and [she]
soon made out that it was the pool of tears s[he]
had wept when she was nine feet high. "I w[ish]
I hadn't cried so much!" said Alice, as s[he]

ABOVE: *Salter's Boat Station in the 1860s. The spot where the historic voyage took off on 4 July 1862 is at the end of Christ Church meadow on the left of the picture. The Head of the River public house now stands near the site, and the name of Salter is still famous on the Thames a century later.*

LEFT: *Alice in the Pool of Tears at Sandford. 'There was a Duck and a Dodo, a Lory and an Eaglet, and several other curious creatures. Alice led the way, and the whole party swam to the shore'. An illustration from the* Facsimile MS Alice.

FACING PAGE, above: *The banks of the Thames near Godstow overlooking Port Meadow where the famous picnic was taken.*

FACING PAGE, below: *A self-portrait of Sir John Tenniel (1820–1914), the Punch artist whose illustrations for the Alice books achieved lasting fame. In* Through the Looking Glass, *the White Knight is clearly the author. From the two drawings it is equally clear that the White Knight was given the features of the illustrator.*

24

imagery of *Through the Looking Glass* relates to the royal celebrations, particularly the bonfire, the Lion and the Unicorn from the royal coat of arms illuminated on so many of the Oxford buildings and the Crown so persistently in Alice's thoughts. Christ Church, as befitted the Royal Foundation and the Prince of Wales's own college, was particularly festive; and high up on the top of the Canterbury gate was a large revolving crown in variegated lamps, which Alice could see from the Deanery upstairs windows.

It was a year when Dodgson was in close contact with the Liddells. He was not always in agreement with the Dean, whom he called a 'relentless reformer', and found himself falling out of favour with Alice's mother on more than one occasion. Mrs Liddell was by all accounts a very outspoken woman, and Dodgson absented himself from the Deanery at the slightest hint of a rebuff. In the Easter vacation of 1863 he had the rare opportunity of being away with the children without their parents, when he was invited over to Charlton Kings, near Cheltenham, by the Dean's mother.

The stories connected with Looking Glass House, the Garden of Live Flowers and the breezy walk above the checkerboard country (the Gloucestershire plain seen from Leckhampton Hill) relate to this visit. A hilarious journey back to Oxford followed with the train jumping over the 'six little brooks' to appear in *Through the Looking Glass*. When the children returned to the Deanery it was to find a new baby brother. His christening was planned to take place during the royal visit in June, with the Prince of Wales standing as godfather to his namesake Albert Edward, but the baby died when only a few weeks old. Charles Dodgson did everything he could to take the children out of the way at this sad and busy time for the Liddells.

A new place to call at was the Bodleian Library, hitherto only open to readers. It was Dean Liddell who encouraged his friend, Henry Coxe, who was the Librarian, to put some of the Bodleian treasures on public display, and early in 1863 the first show cases were put up. In an exhibition on the art of illumination in England the famous Caedmon manuscripts were shown. Tenniel's illustration of the Anglo-Saxon messenger in *Through the Looking Glass* 'With his great hands spread out like fans' records Alice's evident amusement at the extraordinary 'Anglo-Saxon attitudes' of the figures in the Caedmon Genesis.

The Deanery was in a state of turmoil as the royal apartments were prepared. Mr Dodgson took a souvenir photograph of the new royal bedstead, with Alice and her

*   *   *

ABOVE, left: *Dodgson's minute instructions to Macmillans, his publishers, for inserting illustrations in the text of* Alice's Adventures in Wonderland.

ABOVE, right: *Tom Taylor, who introduced Tenniel to Dodgson. He became editor of* Punch *in 1874.*

FACING PAGE: *A page of the original MS of* Alice's Adventures Under Ground. *Dodgson was apparently not satisfied with his drawing of Alice and pasted one of his own photographs of her over it. In the drawing she is seen as the real Alice with black hair cut in a fringe but elsewhere in the book Dodgson gave her a crinkly-haired Pre-Raphaelite look.*

sister sitting importantly on the window seat behind it. Miss Prickett, who is turned into the bossy Red Queen in *Through the Looking Glass*, took upon herself the briefing of the children on behaving suitably in royal presences. 'Curtsey while you're thinking what to say. It saves time. Look up, speak nicely and don't twiddle your fingers all the time,' and above all, 'turn out your toes when you walk – and remember who you are.' Alice's mock banquet was very like the real thing. When she was told that as a royal person in *Through the Looking Glass* she would be required to give a dinner party, she was very relieved on reaching the hall to find everyone already there. 'I'm glad they've come without waiting to be asked,' she thought; 'I should never have known who were the right people to invite.' This was a matter which had exercised the Deanery for weeks before the Christ Church royal banquet. Then there was the business of introductions, protocol and waiting on royal words. Alice had found this aspect rather frightening when as a royal person 'the moment she opened her lips there was dead silence, and all eyes were fixed upon her'. The Christ Church banquet was certainly, as Dodgson recorded in his diary, 'a day to be remembered as unique and most interesting'. For Alice it was the end of the game of Looking Glass World.

The White Knight who had escorted her through the last stage of the game towards the awaited crown was undoubtedly Charles Dodgson himself. Like Dodgson he was 'a great hand at inventing things' and John Tenniel had been given explicit instructions not to make him look old. As Dodgson constantly lamented, 'child friends will grow up so quick', and the time had come for Alice Liddell to take her leave of her White Knight. 'You've only a few yards to go,' he said, 'down the hill and over that little brook, and then you'll be a Queen. But you'll stay and see me off first,' he added as Alice turned away with an eager look. 'I shan't be long. You'll wait and

wave your handkerchief when I get to that turn in the road? I think it'll encourage me, you see.'

There were no more stories and no more outings after the summer of 1863, and on 11 May 1865 Charles Dodgson wrote in his diary: 'Met Alice and Miss Prickett in the quadrangle: Alice seems changed a good deal, and hardly for the better – probably going through the usual awkward stage of transition.' The ideal child-friend had become a dream child, the epitome of childhood and all that the friendship of children would always mean to him. It was with deep emotion that he dedicated the second volume of Alice, *Through the Looking Glass*, published in 1871, to her.

*Child of the pure unclouded
   brow
And dreaming eyes of wonder!
Though time be fleet, and I
   and thou
Are half a life asunder,
Thy loving smile will surely
   hail
The love-gift of a fairy-tale.*

90

of her own little sister. So the boat wound slowly along, beneath the bright summer-day, with its merry crew and its music of voices and laughter, till it passed round one of the many turnings of the stream, and she saw it no more.

Then she thought, (in a dream within the dream, as it were,) how this same little Alice would, in the after-time, be herself a grown woman: and how she would keep, through her riper years, the simple and loving heart of her childhood: and how she would gather around her other little children, and make *their* eyes bright and eager with many a wonderful tale, perhaps even with these very adventures of the little Alice of long-ago: and how she would feel with all their simple sorrows, and find a pleasure in all their simple joys, remembering her own child-life, and the happy summer-days.   days.

27

I have not seen thy sunny face
Nor heard thy silver laughter;
No thought of me shall find
    a place
In thy young life's hereafter –
Enough that now thou wilt not
    fail
To listen to my fairy-tale.

Alice married Reginald Hargreaves who had been at Christ Church from 1872 to 1878. She had very little contact with Charles Dodgson after she moved to Lyndhurst, but in March 1885 he wrote to ask if she would return the manuscript Alice and give her permission to publish the facsimile of it. One of the first copies was sent to Mrs Liddell with the inscription 'To Her whose children's smiles fed the narrator's fancy and were his rich reward'. Duckworth was not forgotten and his copy was inscribed 'The Duck from the Dodo'.

It felt like old times when during a visit to the Deanery in December 1891, Alice received a letter from Mr Dodgson brought across the quad by a messenger.

My Dear Mrs Hargreaves,
    I should be so glad if you could, quite conveniently to yourself, look in for tea any day. You would probably prefer to bring a companion: but I must leave the choice to you, only remarking that, if your husband is here he would be ~~most~~ very welcome (I crossed out "most" because it's ambiguous: most words are I fear) I met him in our Common Room not long ago. It

was hard to realize that he was the husband of one I can scarcely picture to myself even now as more than seven years old.
    Always sincerely,
      Yours   C. L. Dodgson.
Your adventures have had a marvellous success. I have now sold well over 100,000 copies.

Most welcome – the ambiguity of words, a last shy reminder of their old bond in word play nonsense. 'It was such a thunderstorm, you can't think!' (She *never* could, you know said the Red Queen). It was the last occasion on which they met. The Revd Charles Dodgson died on 14 January 1898, while visiting his sisters at Guildford.

Alice Hargreaves did remember all her life those shared experiences and the friendship of the Christ Church mathematics don which had inspired the immortal 'love-gift of a fairy-tale'. It came true, just as her White Knight had fondly hoped it would, and 'years afterwards she could bring the whole scene back again, as if it had been only yesterday – the mild blue eyes and the kindly smile of the Knight – the setting sun gleaming through his hair, and shining on his armour in a blaze of light that quite dazzled her'.

At the age of 80, Alice crossed the Atlantic to be present at the 1932 Lewis Carroll Centenary Celebrations, and when she was awarded an honorary degree for having inspired two great literary

works she replied: 'I feel that Mr Dodgson knows and rejoices with me in the honour that you are

       *   *   *

ABOVE: *Tenniel's illustration for* 'He's an Anglo-Saxon messenger and those are Anglo-Saxon attitudes', *was based on the* Caedmon Genesis *c.1000 (left) in the Bodleian Library.*

FACING PAGE, above: *The Royal visit to Oxford. The Prince and Princess of Wales stayed at the Deanery on 16 June 1863. When the Princess presented prizes to the University Volunteers in Tom Quad, the Liddell children were on the dais (they can be seen under the awning on the left). It was a memorable occasion for Alice.*

FACING PAGE, below left: *Tenniel's illustration recalling the Christ Church Banquet with the ceremonial plate. When Alice cries 'I can't stand this any longer' and pulls the tablecloth off the High Table, the port decanters mysteriously acquire wings and presumably find their way back to the Common Room.*

FACING PAGE, below right: *Queen Alice at what is clearly the door of her father's Chapter House. 'Where's the servant whose business it is to answer the door?' she began angrily. 'Which door?' said the Frog. Alice almost stamped with irritation.... 'This door, of course'.... 'To answer the door?' he said. 'What's it been asking of?' Dodgson's rooms, where he entertained Alice, and her sisters, until he moved in 1862, were nearby.*

soup-ladle was walking up the table to Alice, and signing to her to get out of its way.

" I can't stand this any longer! " she cried, as she

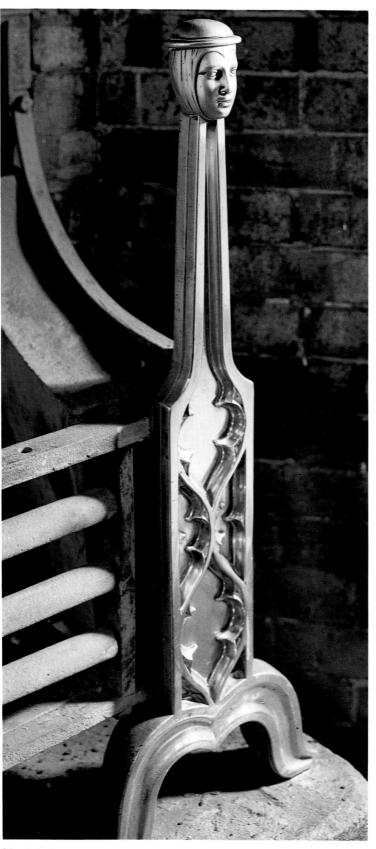

quite du

go on i

        So

soon fir

        *

        "Cu

Alice, (

quite for

"now I'

telescope

feet !" (

at her

out of

far off,

wonder

and sto

I'm sur

deal too

you : yo

way you

to them

they wor

to go !

a new

        A

to herse

doing him.' She afterwards told a reporter that to that most retiring of parsons the ceremony would have seemed as strange as the whimsical stories he used to tell her. 'I wonder how many stories

*   *   *

ABOVE: *The Great Hall, Christ Church, one of the most splendid halls in England. It was finished in 1529 before Wolsey's fall. Cardinal College, which, if completed as Wolsey had intended, would have 'excelled not only all colleges of students but also palaces of princes' was refounded by Henry VIII as Christ Church in 1546. Dodgson once gave a magic lantern show here at a Christmas party for the children of college servants.*

In the fireplaces are brass fire dogs (see facing page) reminiscent of Dodgson's own illustration of Alice with 'an immense length of neck, which seemed to rise like a stalk'.

the world has missed', she added, 'because he never wrote anything down until I teased him into doing it'.

Alice's original manuscript was sold to a collector in the United States, but when it came on the market again, in 1948, it was bought for $50,000 by a group of wellwishers and returned to this country as 'an expression of thanks to a noble people who had held Hitler at bay for a long period single-handed'. It was fitting that it was received in London by the Archbishop of Canterbury before being put on permanent display in the British Museum. At the ceremony the Archbishop called the American gesture of generosity and friendship an 'unsullied and innocent act in a distracted and sinful world'.

Charles Dodgson's portrait hangs in the Great Hall of his col-

lege where he is honoured amongst other famous men of the House – bishops, scholars and prime ministers. Here in the Hall, where Charles Dodgson once told a little girl he had dined 8,000 times, thousands of visitors pause every year before the kind, serious face of the Christ Church don who had captured for all time the wonder of childhood and its unending 'happy summer days'. He had written his nonsense stories 'not for money, and not for fame, but in the hope of supplying, for the children whom I love, some thoughts that may suit those hours of innocent merriment which are the very life of Childhood: and also, in the hope of suggesting to them and to others, some thoughts that may prove, I would fain hope, not wholly out of harmony with the graver cadences of Life'.

ACKNOWLEDGMENTS

The Author is grateful to the Governing Body of Christ Church, and particularly to the Librarian and staff of Christ Church library, the Treasury and the precentor for their help and encouragement; also to the Bodleian Library and Local History section of the Oxford Central Library for assistance in her researches. Special thanks are due to one of the daughters of Augustus Vernon Harcourt for lending her own signed *The Nursery Alice* to be copied for the cover, and to Mrs M. St Clair for allowing publication of Charles Dodgson's last letter to Alice. The illustrations are acknowledged as follows:

Ashmolean Museum, Oxford p. 1 (top); Bodleian Library, Oxford pp. 22, 28 (left); British Library p. 27; Brasenose College, Oxford p. 29 (top); British Museum pp. 24 (bottom), 30 (right); Oxford City Libraries p. 24; Helmut Gernsheim Collection, University of Texas pp. 6 (top right, bottom left and right), 7 (both), 26 (right); Sonia Halliday and Laura Lushington p. 32; Alun Jones pp. 18 (top), 19 (top); Mansell Collection pp, inside front cover, 1 (bottom), 8, 9; Museum of the History of Science, Oxford p. 6; National Portrait Gallery pp. 13, 17 (bottom), 25 (bottom left); S. W. Newbery pp. 2, 20, 31; *The Nursery Alice*, Macmillan front cover; *Alice's Adventures in Wonderland*, Macmillan pp. 19 (bottom), 23 (bottom); *Through the Looking Glass*, Macmillan pp. 18 (bottom), 20 (bottom left), 25 (bottom right), 28 (right), 29 (bottom); J. W. Thomas, Oxford pp. 3 (all), 5, 10 (bottom), 11, 12, 14, 15 (bottom), 16, 17 (top), 21, 23 (top), 26, 30 (left), back cover; Richard Richardson p. 4; Thomas Wilkie, Guildford p. 15.

Sections of the memorial window in All Saints, Daresbury, Cheshire, where Dodgson's father was vicar from 1827–43. As will be seen from the inscription he was born at the parsonage there. The Revd Charles Dodgson moved to St Peter, Croft-on-Tees in 1843, where there is also a memorial to him.

SBN 85372 295 1